90 DAYS DAILY GRATITUDE HABIT JOURNAL

Gratitude Journal for women

FOR MINDFUL HAPPINESS AND POSITIVITY

About the Journal

• • •

Congratulations on your decision to start the Gratitude journalising!

We are grateful that we are able to be a part of your process to live a happier life through this journal. By spending 3 to 5 minutes daily, this 90 days guided gratitude journal will help you live a happier, healthier and successful life.

Goal of this journal is to make gratitude a natural habit where you will no longer require any external tools.

Gratitude journalising should be praticed **deliberately** with a relaxed mind preferably when you wake up or before you sleep. This journal is designed in a such way that by the end of 90 days you will start enjoying even the smallest events around you.

Happy Gratituding!!

• • •

If you love our book, feel free to leave a review. :)

What is Gratitude?

To put it in simple terms. **Gratitude is nothing but feeling thankful for all the positives in our life.** No matter how small or big they are. This might be overlooked by many as being a silly thing to do.

Having an attitude of gratitude doesn't cost any money. It doesn't take much time. But the benefits of gratitude are enormous.

What science says about Gratitude?

Several studies indicate that practicing gratitude improves our life/happiness by up to 10%. People after **deliberate** guided practice of gratitude for a few months seems to yield the benefits.

Positive psychology research has shown that gratitude touches on many aspects of our lives. Our emotions. Personality. Social dynamics. Career success and health. All of these plays an important role in increasing our basic happiness.

Some Benefits of Gratitude

- Gratitude increases happiness even it is as less of five minutes.
- Gratitude attracts people around us making relationships even stronger.
- Gratitude makes us more healthier.
- Gratitude makes us even more effiicent in our careers.
- Gratitude strengthens our positive emotions.
- Gratitude increase spirtual transcendence.
- Gratitude makes us less self-centered.

Pictorial representation of Benefits

HEALTH
LESS STRESS
BETTER SLEEP
MORE ENERGY

RELATIONSHIPS
MORE KINDNESS
MORE FRIENDS
STRONGER MARRI-
GAGE

CAREER
ACHIEVE GOALS
BETTER FOCUS
MORE PRODUCTIVE

Happiness

EMOTIONAL
MORE RELAXED
LESS ENVIOUS
MORE GOOD FEELING

PERSONALITY
LESS SELF CENTERED
MORE OPTIMISTIC
MORE SPIRITUAL

Progress Exercise

Before you start this book, try completing this small excercise

Look around your room and describe about few things you see...

....
....
....
....
....
....
....
....

Look through the window and describe the few things you notice...

....
....
....
....
....
....
....
....
....
....
....

Today I'm Thankful for...

....

....

....

....

....

....

....

....

....

Smallest thing I enjoyed today...

....

....

....

....

....

....

The Best part of today was...

66

No one is perfect – that's why pencils have erasers.

– Wolfgang Riebe

99

Today I'm Thankful for....

....
....
....
....
....
....
....
....

Smallest thing I enjoyed today...

....
....
....
....
....

One family member I am grateful for is...

Today I'm Thankful for...

....

....

....

....

....

....

....

....

Smallest thing I enjoyed today...

....

....

....

....

....

One freedom I often take it for granted is...

Today I'm Thankful for....

....
....
....
....
....
....
....
....

Smallest thing I enjoyed today...

....
....
....
....
....
....

One skill I'm most grateful for is...

66

Positive thinking will let you do everything better than negative thinking
will.

– Zig Ziglar 99

Today I'm Thankful for...

....
....
....
....
....
....
....
....
....

Smallest thing I enjoyed today...

....
....
....
....
....

One person who always inspires me is...

66

Keep your face to the sunshine and you cannot see a shadow.

- Helen Keller

99

Today I'm Thankful for....

....
....
....
....
....
....
....
....
....

Smallest thing I enjoyed today...

....
....
....
....
....
....

I am so thankful to my parents for...

66

In every day, there are 1,440 minutes. That means we have 1,440 daily
opportunities to make a positive impact.

– Les Brown

99

Today I'm Thankful for...

....
....
....
....
....
....
....
....
....

Smallest thing I enjoyed today...

....
....
....
....
....

One part in my body I love the most...

"
When you are enthusiastic about what you do, you feel this positive
energy. It's very simple.
- Paulo Coelho
"

Today I'm Thankful for....

....
....
....
....
....
....
....
....

Smallest thing I enjoyed today...

....
....
....
....
....

I'm gratefful for my following beliefs and faiths...

66

Positive anything is better than negative nothing.

- Elbert Hubbard

99

Today I'm Thankful for...

....
....
....
....
....
....
....
....
....
....

Smallest thing I enjoyed today...

....
....
....
....
....
....

One thing I love the most about my spouse...

> In order to carry a positive action, we must develop here a positive vision.
>
> – Dalai Lama

Today I'm Thankful for....

....
....
....
....
....
....
....

Smallest thing I enjoyed today...

....
....
....
....
....

Most favorite part of the place I live in is...

"
Virtually nothing is impossible in this world if you just put your mind to it
and maintain a positive attitude.

– Lou Holtz
"

Today I'm Thankful for...

....
....
....
....
....
....
....
....

Smallest thing I enjoyed today...

....
....
....
....
....

One thing I appreciate the most about my job/work...

> **"**
> Optimism is a happiness magnet. If you stay positive good things and good people will be drawn to you.
>
> – Mary Lou Retton **"**

Today I'm Thankful for....

Smallest thing I enjoyed today...

I'm grateful for my favorite animals or pets because...

"
It makes a big difference in your life when you stay positive.

- Ellen DeGeneres "

Today I'm Thankful for...

Smallest thing I enjoyed today...

The one thing I did today that I couldn't do yesterday...

> Happiness is an attitude. We either make ourselves miserable, or happy and strong. The amount of work is the same.
>
> – Francesca Reigler

Today I'm Thankful for....

....
....
....
....
....
....
....
....

Smallest thing I enjoyed today...

....
....
....
....
....
....

The best birthday I ever had was...

66

The sun himself is weak when he first rises, and gathers strength and courage as the day gets on.

— Charles Dickens

99

Today I'm Thankful for...

....
....
....
....
....
....
....

Smallest thing I enjoyed today...

....
....
....
....
....

The one song I love the most is...

66
The way I see it, if you want the rainbow, you gotta put up with
the rain.

– Dolly Parton
99

Today I'm Thankful for....

Smallest thing I enjoyed today...

One vacation I enjoyed the most was...

"
Every day may not be good... but there's something good in every day.

- Alice Morse Earle
"

Today I'm Thankful for...

....
....
....
....
....
....
....
....
....

Smallest thing I enjoyed Today...

....
....
....
....
....

The Teachers whom I'm grateful for are...

66

You cannot have a positive life and a negative mind.

- Joyce Meyer

99

Today I'm Thankful for....

....
....
....
....
....
....
....
....

Smallest thing I enjoyed today...

....
....
....
....
....
....

One positive aspect of my favorite weather condition...

66

The more you praise and celebrate your life. the more there is in life to celebrate.

– Oprah Winfrey 99

Today I'm Thankful for...

Smallest thing I enjoyed today...

One reason I'm grateful for my safety...

" Be thankful for everything that happens in your life: it's all an experience

– Roy T Bennet **"**

Today I'm Thankful for....

....
....
....
....
....
....
....
....
....

Smallest thing I enjoyed today...

....
....
....
....
....
....

The reason I'm thankful for my favorite food is...

66

Wherever you go. no matter what the weather. always bring your own
sunshine.

- Anthony J. D'Angelo

99

Today I'm Thankful for...

....
....
....
....
....
....
....
....
....

Smallest thing I enjoyed today...

....
....
....
....
....

One Book which meant a lot to me till date...

> **66**
>
> If you want light to come into your life. you need to stand where it is shining.
>
> – Guy Finley **99**

Today I'm Thankful for....

....
....
....
....
....
....
....
....

Smallest thing I enjoyed today...

....
....
....
....
....

My most valueable and worthwhile purchase is...

66

Happiness is the only thing that multiplies when you share it.

- Albert Schweitzer 99

Today I'm Thankful for...

....
....
....
....
....
....
....
....
....

Smallest thing I enjoyed today...

....
....
....
....
....

One of the most valueable life lesson I learnt is...

66

The happiness of your life depends upon the quality of your thoughts.

- Marcus Aurelius

99

Today I'm Thankful for....

....
....
....
....
....
....
....
....
....

Smallest thing I enjoyed today...

....
....
....
....
....

Promise that I made and kept till now...

“
A truly happy person is one who can enjoy the scenery while on
a detour.

- Anonymous
”

Today I'm Thankful for...

....
....
....
....
....
....
....
....
....
....

Smallest thing I enjoyed today...

....
....
....
....
....
....

The one person to whom I showed mercy...

66
Be so happy that, when other people look at you, they become happy too.

- Anonymous
99

Today I'm Thankful for....

....
....
....
....
....
....
....
....
....

Smallest thing I enjoyed today...

....
....
....
....
....
....

The one friend I cherish the most...

66

Live life to the fullest and focus on the positive.

– Matt Cameron

99

Today I'm Thankful for...

....
....
....
....
....
....
....
....
....

Smallest thing I enjoyed today...

....
....
....
....
....

One simple pleasure that I value is...

" Start each day with a positive thought and a grateful heart.

- Roy T Bennett **"**

Today I'm Thankful for....

....
....
....
....
....
....
....
....

Smallest thing I enjoyed today...

....
....
....
....
....

The authors I get inspired the most are...

"
Always turn a negative situation into a positive situation

- Micheal Jordan "

Today I'm Thankful for...

....
....
....
....
....
....
....
....

Smallest thing I enjoyed today...

....
....
....
....
....

My favorite movie is... One reason I love it the most is...

66

I always like to look on the optimistic side of life, but I am realistic
enough to know that life is a complex matter.

- Walt Disney

99

Today I'm Thankful for....

....
....
....
....
....
....
....
....
....

Smallest thing I enjoyed today...

....
....
....
....
....

One thing I appreciate the most about myself is...

"

Every positive value has its price in negative terms... the genius of
Einstein leads to Hiroshima.

- Pablo Picasso **"**

Today I'm Thankful for...

....
....
....
....
....
....
....
....
....

Smallest thing I enjoyed today...

....
....
....
....
....

My favorite color is... One reason I love it the most...

66
I always like to look on the optimistic side of life, but I am realistic
enough to know that life is a complex matter.

- Walt Disney
99

Today I'm Thankful for....

....
....
....
....
....
....
....
....
....

Smallest thing I enjoyed today...

....
....
....
....
....
....

One moment which made me to laugh the most...

66

I've always believed that you can think positive just as well as you can think negative.

- James Baldwin

99

Today I'm Thankful for...

....
....
....
....
....
....
....
....
....

Smallest thing I enjoyed today...

....
....
....
....
....

One technology I'm grateful for is...

"

Pessimism leads to weakness. optimism to power.

- William James

"

Today I'm Thankful for....

....
....
....
....
....
....
....
....

Smallest thing I enjoyed today...

....
....
....
....
....

One childhood event for which I'm thankful for is...

66

My dear friend, clear your mind of cant.

- Samuel Johnson

99

Today I'm Thankful for...

....
....
....
....
....
....
....
....
....

Smallest thing I enjoyed today...

....
....
....
....
....

My favorite place in my home is...

66

The most positive men are the most credulous.

- Alexander Pope

99

Today I'm Thankful for....

....
....
....
....
....
....
....
....

Smallest thing I enjoyed today...

....
....
....
....
....

The one reason I'm grateful for this tough situation I faced...

> It takes but one positive thought when given a chance to survive and thrive to overpower an entire army of negative thoughts.
>
> – Robert H. Schuller

Today I'm Thankful for...

....
....
....
....
....
....
....
....

Smallest thing I enjoyed today...

....
....
....
....
....

Three Things that makes me smile instantly are...

> 66 Positive thinking is more than just a tagline. It changes the way we be-
> have. And I firmly believe that when I am positive, it not only makes me
> better, but it also makes those around me better.
> - Harvey Mackay 99

Today I'm Thankful for....

....
....
....
....
....
....
....
....
....

Smallest thing I enjoyed today...

....
....
....
....
....

One reason why I'm grateful for this daily routine is...

66

When someone does something good, applaud! You will make two people happy.

– Samuel Goldwyn

99

Today I'm Thankful for...

....
....
....
....
....
....
....
....

Smallest thing I enjoyed today...

....
....
....
....
....

The one smell/scent that always gives me pleasure is...

66

A lot of times people look at the negative side of what they feel they
can't do. I always look on the positive side of what I can do.

- Chuck Norris

99

Today I'm Thankful for....

....
....
....
....
....
....
....
....

Smallest thing I enjoyed today...

....
....
....
....
....

The one lifestyle habit that I'm grateful for is...

66

The learner always begins by finding fault. but the scholar sees the
positive merit in everything.

- Georg Wilhelm Friedrich Hegel

99

Today I'm Thankful for...

....
....
....
....
....
....
....
....

Smallest thing I enjoyed today...

....
....
....
....
....

I admire these three habits of my grandparents...

66
That's my gift. I let that negativity roll off me like water off a duck's back.
If it's not positive. I didn't hear it. If you can overcome that, fights are
easy.   - George Foreman   99

Today I'm Thankful for....

....
....
....
....
....
....
....
....
....

Smallest thing I enjoyed today...

....
....
....
....
....
....

One surprise that I will cherish the rest of my life is...

66

I like to encourage people to realize that any action is a good action if it's
proactive and there is positive intent behind it.

- Micheal J. Fox

99

Today I'm Thankful for...

....
....
....
....
....
....
....
....

Smallest thing I enjoyed today...

....
....
....
....
....

One event from the past you are grateful for is...

" It's a wonderful thing to be optimistic. It keeps you healthy and it keeps you resilient.

- Daniel Kahneman **"**

Today I'm Thankful for....

....
....
....
....
....
....
....
....
....

Smallest thing I enjoyed today...

....
....
....
....
....

One reason I'm excited for this future event is...

66

Live life to the fullest, and focus on the positive.

- Matt Cameron

99

Today I'm Thankful for...

....
....
....
....
....
....
....
....
....

Smallest thing I enjoyed today...

....
....
....
....
....

Things I consider luxuries for which I'm grateful for are...

66
A strong, positive self image is the best possible preparation for success.

- Joyce Brothers
99

Today I'm Thankful for....

....
....
....
....
....
....
....
....

Smallest thing I enjoyed today...

....
....
....
....
....

One reason I love this planet...

" Say and do something positive that will help the situation; it doesn't take any brains to complain.

– Robert A. Cook **"**

Today I'm Thankful for...

Smallest thing I enjoyed today...

Three things that comforts me are...

Today I'm Thankful for....

....
....
....
....
....
....
....
....
....

Smallest thing I enjoyed today...

....
....
....
....
....

Modes of transportation for which I'm thankful for are...

66
I think anything is possible if you have the mindset and the will and
desire to do it and put the time in.

- Roger Clemens
99

Today I'm Thankful for...

....
....
....
....
....
....
....
....

Smallest thing I enjoyed today...

....
....
....
....
....

I'm grateful for this system in my body for supporting my life...

66

Fortune cookies are a good idea. If the message is positive, it can make your day a little better.

- Yao Ming

99

Today I'm Thankful for....

....
....
....
....
....
....
....
....
....

Smallest thing I enjoyed today...

....
....
....
....
....

I'm grateful for this human invention...

" I think a lot of times we don't pay enough attention to people with a positive attitude because we assume they are naive or stupid or unschooled.

– Amy Adams **"**

Today I'm Thankful for...

....
....
....
....
....
....
....
....
....

Smallest thing I enjoyed today...

....
....
....
....
....

One natural phenomenon I love the most is...

66
Instead of hating. I have chosen to forgive and spend all of my positive
energy on changing the world.

- Camryn Manheim
99

Today I'm Thankful for....

....
....
....
....
....
....
....
....

Smallest thing I enjoyed today...

....
....
....
....
....

I'm grateful for this person for my financial abundance...

" A positive attitude is something everyone can work on. and everyone can learn how to employ it.

– Joan Lunden **"**

Today I'm Thankful for...

....
....
....
....
....
....
....
....

Smallest thing I enjoyed today...

....
....
....
....
....

One kind activity someone did for me recently...

66

I am fascinated by what is beautiful, strong, healthy, what is living. I seek harmony.

- Leni Rienfenstahl

99

Today I'm Thankful for....

....
....
....
....
....
....
....
....
....

Smallest thing I enjoyed today...

....
....
....
....
....
....

I'm thankful for this person who always listens to me when I Talk...

“ A positive attitude causes a chain reaction of positive thoughts, events
and outcomes. It is a catalyst and it sparks extraordinary results.

- Wade Boggs ”

Today I'm Thankful for...

Smallest thing I enjoyed today...

Three websites for which I'm thankful are...

" I have never, ever focused on the negative of things. I always look at the positive. "

- Sonia Sotomayor

Today I'm Thankful for....

....
....
....
....
....
....
....
....
....

Smallest thing I enjoyed today...

....
....
....
....
....

Recent public event I enjoyed the most is...

66

Choosing to be positive and having a grateful attitude is going to deter-
mine how you're going to live your life.

– Joel Osteen **99**

Today I'm Thankful for...

Smallest thing I enjoyed today...

Three modern day medicines for which I'm grateful are...

" Virtually nothing is impossible in this world if you just put your mind to it and maintain a positive attitude.

- Lou Holtz "

Today I'm Thankful for....

....
....
....
....
....
....
....
....

Smallest thing I enjoyed today...

....
....
....
....
....

The small help which I did made someone happy was...

Today I'm Thankful for...

....
....
....
....
....
....
....
....

Smallest thing I enjoyed today...

....
....
....
....
....

One recent creative idea of mine I enjoyed the most was...

66

Be not afraid of life. Believe that life is worth living. and your belief will help create the fact.

- William James

99

Today I'm Thankful for....

....
....
....
....
....
....
....
....
....

Smallest thing I enjoyed today...

....
....
....
....
....

One sound of the nature I'm grateful for is...

" Stay positive in every situation and everything you do, never stop trying,
have faith don't stop due to failure.

- Anurag Prakash Ray "

Today I'm Thankful for...

....
....
....
....
....
....
....
....
....

Smallest thing I enjoyed today...

....
....
....
....
....

I'm grateful for this one gadget...

66

Believe you can and you're halfway there.

- Theodore Roosevelt

99

Today I'm Thankful for....

....
....
....
....
....
....
....
....
....

Smallest thing I enjoyed today...

....
....
....
....
....

My Favorite photo is... One reason I love it the most is...

66

Optimism is a happiness magnet. If you stay positive, good things and
good people will be drawn to you.

– Mary Lou Retton

99

Today I'm Thankful for...

Smallest thing I enjoyed today...

One reason I enjoy this birds sound...

" You have to be positive. and I'm not just talking about athletics. this also applies to life.

– Sheryl Swoopes

Today I'm Thankful for....

....
....
....
....
....
....
....
....

Smallest thing I enjoyed today...

....
....
....
....
....

One reason I'm grateful for these clothes or jewelry...

" Focus on your strengths, not your weaknesses. Focus on your character,
not your reputation. Focus on your blessings, not your misfortunes.

— Roy T. Bennett "

Today I'm Thankful for...

....
....
....
....
....
....
....
....
....

Smallest thing I enjoyed today...

....
....
....
....
....

One reason I'm grateful for this holiday is...

" Dwell on the beauty of life. Watch the stars, and see yourself running with
them.

"

- Marcus Aurelius

Today I'm Thankful for....

....
....
....
....
....
....
....
....
....

Smallest thing I enjoyed today...

....
....
....
....
....

My favorite quote... One reason I'm grateful for it is...

" Love yourself. It is important to stay positive because beauty comes
from the inside out.

- Jenn Proske "

Today I'm Thankful for...

....
....
....
....
....
....
....
....
....

Smallest thing I enjoyed today...

....
....
....
....
....
....

One emotion that I love to experience is...

> **Life is 10% what happens to us and 90% how we react to it.**
>
> **- Dennis P. Kimbro**

Today I'm Thankful for....

....
....
....
....
....
....
....
....
....

Smallest thing I enjoyed today...

....
....
....
....
....

The best hug I received/gave was...

" Be positive with every idea surrounding your dreams. Think about the possibility of what you plan to do and approach it with an optimistic action. Stay positively. **"**

– Israelmore Ayivor

Today I'm Thankful for...

....
....
....
....
....
....
....
....

Smallest thing I enjoyed today...

....
....
....
....
....

The three positive things that are in front of me right now...

> 66 If you have a positive attitude and constantly strive to give your best effort, eventually you will overcome your immediate problems and find you are ready for greater challenges.
>
> – Pat Riley 99

Today I'm Thankful for....

....
....
....
....
....
....
....
....
....

Smallest thing I enjoyed today...

....
....
....
....
....

One way I'm better today than I was one year ago is...

66

If you are positive, you'll see opportunities instead of obstacles.

- Widad Akrawi

99

Today I'm Thankful for...

....
....
....
....
....
....
....
....

Smallest thing I enjoyed today...

....
....
....
....
....

An everyday item that I depend on but rarely grateful for is...

Today I'm Thankful for....

....
....
....
....
....
....
....
....

Smallest thing I enjoyed today...

....
....
....
....
....

I'm thanful for this one life hack I learnt recently...

" Nothing makes a person happier than having a happy heart.

- Roy T. Bennett "

Today I'm Thankful for...

....
....
....
....
....
....
....
....
....

Smallest thing I enjoyed today...

....
....
....
....
....

I'm grateful for this in-born talent of mine...

66
The more you are positive and say. 'I want to have a good life.' the more
you build that reality for yourself by creating the life that you want.

99
- Chris Pine

Today I'm Thankful for....

....
....
....
....
....
....
....
....
....

Smallest thing I enjoyed today...

....
....
....
....
....

One of the best things about being married/single/in relationship...

"
The thing that lies at the foundation of positive change. the way I see it.
is service to a fellow human being.

- Lee Lacocca
"

Today I'm Thankful for...

....

....

....

....

....

....

....

....

Smallest thing I enjoyed today...

....

....

....

....

....

Three things I'm grateful about mornings are...

66

Attitude is a little thing that makes a big difference.

99

- Winston Churchill

Today I'm Thankful for....

....
....
....
....
....
....
....
....

Smallest thing I enjoyed today...

....
....
....
....
....
....

Three Things I'm grateful about nights are...

66 The worst times can be the best if you think with positive energy.

– Domenico Dolce 99

Today I'm Thankful for...

....
....
....
....
....
....
....
....

Smallest thing I enjoyed today...

....
....
....
....
....

I'm very proud of this one thing in my life....

66

Live each day as if your life had just begun.

- Johann Wolfgang Von Goethe 99

Today I'm Thankful for....

....
....
....
....
....
....
....
....
....

Smallest thing I enjoyed today...

....
....
....
....
....

My favorite month is... The reason I love it the most is...

> "Having a positive mental attitude is asking how something can be done rather than saying it can't be done.
>
> - Bo Bennett

Today I'm Thankful for...

....

....

....

....

....

....

....

....

....

Smallest thing I enjoyed today...

....

....

....

....

....

I'm grateful for this passion of mine..

66

Inspiration comes from within yourself. One has to be positive. When you're positive. good things happen.

– Deep Roy

99

Today I'm Thankful for....

....
....
....
....
....
....
....
....
....

Smallest thing I enjoyed today...

....
....
....
....
....
....

I was appreciated/praised for this event recently...

Today I'm Thankful for...

....
....
....
....
....
....
....
....
....

Smallest thing I enjoyed today...

....
....
....
....
....

Three reasons I'm grateful for sleep are...

> **"** You can't make positive choices for the rest of your life without an environment that makes those choices easy, natural, and enjoyable. **"**
>
> **- Deepak Chopra**

Today I'm Thankful for....

....
....
....
....
....
....
....
....

Smallest thing I enjoyed today...

....
....
....
....

One reason I enjoy eating this dessert is...

66

Live your days on the positive side of life. in tune with your most trea-
sured values. And in each moment you'll have much to live for.

– Ralph Marston

99

Today I'm Thankful for...

....
....
....
....
....
....
....
....

Smallest thing I enjoyed today...

....
....
....
....
....

I'm grateful for this surprise visit I made recently...

66

Positive energy knows no boundaries. If everyone were to spread positive energy on the Internet, the world would be a much better place.

- Lu Wei

99

Today I'm Thankful for....

....
....
....
....
....
....
....
....

Smallest thing I enjoyed today...

....
....
....
....
....

I'm grateful for this event which made me to quit a bad habit...

66

Adopting a really positive attitude can work wonders to adding years to
your life. a spring to your step. a sparkle to your eye. and all of that.

- Christie Brinkley

99

Today I'm Thankful for...

....
....
....
....
....
....
....
....
....

Smallest thing I enjoyed today...

....
....
....
....
....

The one person whom I think owe a thank you...

> **"** Positive culture comes from being mindful, and respecting your coworkers, and being empathetic. **"**
>
> - Biz Stone

Today I'm Thankful for....

....
....
....
....
....
....
....
....

Smallest thing I enjoyed today...

....
....
....
....
....

This is how I feel whenever I see a rainbow...

> Take your mind off the problems for a moment. and focus on the positive possibilities. Consider how very much you are able to do.
>
> - Ralph Marston

Today I'm Thankful for...

....
....
....
....
....
....
....
....

Smallest thing I enjoyed today...

....
....
....
....
....

My favorite flower is...One reason I love it the most is...

> You can do everything you can to try to stop bad things from happening to you, but eventually things will happen, so the best prevention is a positive attitude.
> — Marie Osmond

Today I'm Thankful for....

....
....
....
....
....
....
....
....

Smallest thing I enjoyed today...

....
....
....
....
....

One huge thing that I learnt last year...

Today I'm Thankful for...

....
....
....
....
....
....
....
....
....

Smallest thing I enjoyed today...

....
....
....
....
....

I'm grateful for this weakness of mine as it helped me to grow...

66
I will keep smiling, be positive and never give up! I will give 100 percent
each time I play. These are always my goals and my attitude.

99

- Yani Tseng

Today I'm Thankful for...

....
....
....
....
....
....
....
....

Smallest thing I enjoyed today...

....
....
....
....
....

Three things that changed after I started practising gratitude...

66

Stay positive and happy. Work hard and don't give up hope. Be open to
criticism and keep learning. Surround yourself with happy, warm and
genuine people.

99

— Tena Desae

Progress Exercise

Look around your room and describe few of those...

....

....

....

....

....

....

....

....

Look through the window and describe the few things you notice...

....

....

....

....

....

....

....

....

....

....

Compare this writing with the progress excercise you completed before you
started this journal and try measuring your progress.

Made in United States
Cleveland, OH
20 May 2025

17051083R00056